The World of Martial Arts

Karate

By Jim Ollhoff

Visit us at
www.abdopublishing.com

Published by ABDO Publishing Company, 8000 West 78th Street, Suite 310, Edina, MN 55439.
Copyright ©2008 by Abdo Consulting Group, Inc. International copyrights reserved in all countries.
No part of this book may be reproduced in any form without written permission from the publisher.
ABDO & Daughters™ is a trademark and logo of ABDO Publishing Company.

Printed in the United States.

Editor: John Hamilton
Graphic Design: John Hamilton
Cover Design: Neil Klinepier
Cover Illustration: iStockphoto
Interior Photos and Illustrations: p 1 woman kicking bag, iStockphoto; p 5 woman kicking, Getty Images; p 6 man kicking in front of rising sun, AP Images; p 7 map of Okinawa, CIA; p 8 samurai, iStockphoto; p 9 woman with kamas, iStockphoto; p 9 (inset) farmer with tool, Corbis; p 10 Masatoshi Nakayama, Getty Images; p 11 ships on Okinawan beach, Getty Images; p 12 colored belts, iStockphoto; p 13 karate kids, Getty Images; p 15 man performing kata, Getty Images; p 17 man breaking board, Getty Images; p 18 man making fist, Getty Images; p 19 woman demonstrating knife hand, iStockphoto; p 20 (top) man blocking kick with upblock, Getty Images; p 20 (bottom) woman demonstrates downblock, iStockphoto; p 21 woman demonstrates front kick, iStockphoto; p 22 woman demonstrates round kick, iStockphoto; p 23 man demonstrates side kick, iStockphoto; p 25 tae kwon do women sparring, Getty Images; p 26 man demonstrates flying side kick, Getty Images; p 27 tae kwon do sparring action from Athens Olympics, Getty Images; p 28 karate students practice on beach, iStockphoto; p 29 woman karate student demonstrates kata, Getty Images; p 31 woman demonstrates side kick, iStockphoto.

Library of Congress Cataloging-in-Publication Data

Ollhoff, Jim, 1959-
    Karate / Jim Ollhoff.
        p. cm. -- (The world of martial arts)
    Includes index.
    ISBN 978-1-59928-977-9
    1. Karate--Juvenile literature. I. Title.

    GV1114.3.O55 2008
    796.815'3--dc22

                            2007030547

CONTENTS

KARATE

Martial arts is a term for all the fighting styles combined. There are thousands of styles, each with different philosophies. The styles have different defenses and different ideas about fighting. Various systems of fighting come from all over the world.

One of the most popular systems of martial arts is called *karate*. It began more than 400 years ago on Okinawa, the largest island in the Ryukyu chain of islands in the Pacific Ocean. (Today, Okinawa and the Ryukyu chain of islands are the southernmost prefecture, or state, of Japan.) Okinawa had frequent visitors and settlers from Japan and China. This interchange of cultures played a big part in the development of karate.

Within karate, there are hundreds of styles. Some of the most common styles are shorin-ryu karate, gojo-ryu karate, kenpo karate, and shotokan karate. There is no group or organization that controls karate, or decides which styles should be included. Therefore, a karate expert can create a new style at any time. In fact, this has happened continuously since the beginning of karate—people start a new style, give it a name, and start teaching it.

The word karate means "empty hand." Those who practice karate, called *karatekas*, train for long hours over many years. Only a small percentage of people who begin training will finish with a black belt—the symbol of expertise in karate.

Left: Karate is famous for its powerful punches and kicks.

Some martial arts of the world are known for their speed. Other martial arts are known for acrobatic kicks, or for their expert use of weapons. The one word that might describe karate is "power." Karate is known for powerful punches and kicks. Karatekas have strong, wide stances that help them strike with more power. Karatekas like to have attacks so strong that they can knock someone down with a single punch. This is one of the reasons they practice breaking boards. Breaking a board or a block of cement is practice for the one-punch knockouts that karatekas enjoy.

HISTORY OF KARATE

It is hard to know the complete history of karate in Okinawa. We have many legends about the beginnings of karate, but very few facts. We have lots of stories, but we don't know for sure how many of them are true. There are a couple of reasons that the history of karate is cloudy.

For hundreds of years, karate was kept a strict secret. A master taught a few students, but he swore them to secrecy. They could not practice in public or show anyone their techniques. In fact, they could not even tell anyone that they were studying karate. The secrecy began to lift at the end of the 1800s, but by then much of the knowledge of history had been lost. The secrecy lifted completely in 1904, when Okinawans began to teach karate in their public schools.

Right: Early karate masters kept their techniques secret. Many stories and legends sprang up that tell of the origins of this martial art.

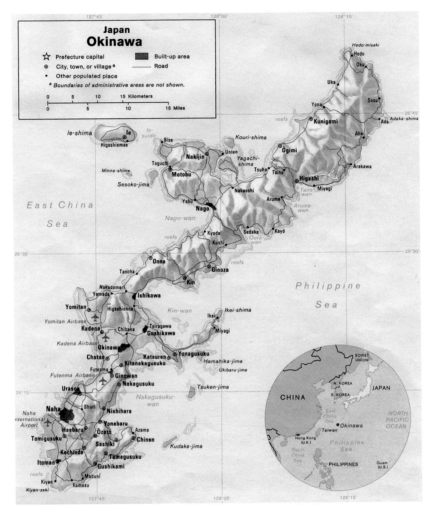

Left: A map of the southern Japanese island of Okinawa, which is part of the Ryukyu chain of islands.

There is another reason why the history of karate is murky. It has to do with stories that people invent. Legends always spring up when there is a lack of knowledge. In Okinawa, because of the secrecy, legends have sprung up about the origins of karate. Sometimes it is difficult to sort out which legends are true or false. Some legends are partially true. Other legends are false, but use a real person in the story. All the legends make it difficult for historians to figure out exactly what happened.

Here is the most often-told legend for the origins of karate in Okinawa: The Japanese invaded Okinawa in 1609. According to this legend, the Japanese forbade anyone to own a weapon. People could not own swords, daggers, bows and arrows, or firearms. Anyone caught with a weapon was severely punished. The Okinawans were left with only their bare hands and feet, and had to learn how to use them to defend themselves. Since they had no weapons, they had to use simple farming tools for self-defense. The Okinawan farmers used a seed planter called a sai, which became a very effective tool to defend against swords. They had a rice gatherer called a nunchaku, which became an effective offensive weapon. The Okinawans already had a primitive martial art called *te*, meaning "hands." The Okinawan te masters and Chinese kung fu masters blended their skills into a new martial art called *kara-te* or "empty hands." This is the legend of the origin of Okinawan karate.

We know that at least parts of this legend are true. We know that the Japanese Satsuma clan did indeed invade Okinawa in 1609, in part to punish the Okinawans for refusing to give Japan supplies they needed in their war with China a few years earlier. We know that there was an Okinawan art called te, although it's unclear whether it was a martial art or a native dance. We know that many Chinese lived on the island. Chinese had lived in Okinawa since at least 1393 A.D., and probably much earlier. It may be that Chinese kung fu masters brought their art to Okinawa at that time.

Above: A legend about the origin of karate says that invading Japanese samurai forbade Okinawans from using weapons. The Okinawans learned to use their hands and feet to defend themselves.

Above: The kama is a weapon with a curved blade on the end of a wooden handle. It may have its origins as an Asian tool for harvesting crops (inset).

Below: Masatoshi Nakayama, an 8th dan black belt and chief instructor of the Japan Karate Association, in 1968.

It's unclear, if it happened at all, whether the Japanese outlawed all weapons, or just military weapons. The idea of peace-loving Okinawans picking up farming tools and learning to use them as weapons is a fun idea. However, it's clear that the Okinawans were not the first people to invent these karate weapons. The Chinese had been using weapons of this type for hundreds of years.

The exact way that karate started has been lost to us. It may be that karate, as we know it today, did not develop until the middle 1800s. However, it's clear that by the late 1800s, karate became an effective and well-developed fighting style.

Many U.S. servicemen lived and worked in Okinawa during and after World War II, which ended in 1945.

These servicemen were exposed to karate during that time, and some men learned karate while they were there. The first karate school in the United States was opened in Phoenix, Arizona, in 1946 by Robert Trias.

By the 1960s, tournaments in the United States had become popular as a way for karate stylists to demonstrate their skills. Television and movies began to popularize karate, moving it into the American mainstream.

Above: Ships deliver supplies and equipment on an Okinawan beach during the U.S. occupation of the island in World War II.

Uniforms and Belts

Karate students wear a uniform called a *gi*. It is usually white, and is very loose fitting. The pants are loose enough to do kicks. The top is usually a loose jacket tied off at the hips. Recently, some karate schools have begun wearing designer uniforms, with colored uniforms and school emblems.

Usually, students practice in bare feet. Down through history, karatekas practiced this way. It gives students a better feel for the floor when they have to make wide stances or keep their balance on one leg.

In the early karate days in Okinawa, karatekas wore a belt that would hold their jacket to their body. The belt was a long, heavy cloth belt. Students would wrap it around the body twice and tie it in the front. In the early days, all the belts were white. The more years a person practiced, the dirtier their belt became. Students learned to respect the people who had dirtier, darker belts. According to legend, this is the origin of the black belt. The most experienced students had the blackest belts. This is a popular legend, but historians are not sure if it is true.

Below: Belt rankings vary among karate schools, but the most inexperienced students usually wear white belts, while the most advanced students wear black belts.

Left: Young students at a karate school, with various colored belt rankings.

Today, most karate schools have a ranking system with belt colors. Most students start with a white belt when they join a school. As they become more experienced, they take tests to prove to the instructor what they know. When the students pass a test, they receive a new belt of a higher color.

Each school has a different ranking system. A red belt may be a beginner in one school, and be close to a black belt in another school. Usually, white and gold belts represent the beginners. Blue and green belts represent the middle students, and brown belts represent the more advanced students. Black is usually the final color, although black belts continue to learn and take tests. When they receive their black belt, they are a 1st *dan*, or 1st rank. Their next rank is 2nd dan, and then 3rd dan, and so on. Typically, the highest in a karate style is 10th dan. By that time, they have studied karate for decades, and are often so elderly that the title is an honorary one.

KATA

Most karate styles practice a series of movements called a *kata,* or form. A kata is a pre-arranged series of movements done to practice techniques. It is 20, 30, or more separate punches or kicks, done crisply, quickly, and powerfully. It is almost like a dance. Each movement is a technique done against an imaginary attacker—a punch, a block, an attack, or defense. Kata is one of the most important parts of karate training. Students practice katas over and over in order to make them perfect.

When performing a kata, students imagine that 20 or more people are attacking, one right after another. Through practice, students train themselves to do the techniques properly. They can practice doing it stronger and faster. They can get better and better at doing the techniques powerfully. Students must practice their kata until they can do it perfectly. They must do it from memory, and do it with confidence and control.

Most katas begin with the student standing at attention, and then bowing to the instructor as a sign of respect. The student executes the first movement, then freezes in place. The second move is executed. The student freezes again. The entire kata is executed quickly and strongly, but there is a slight pause between each movement.

Usually, beginning students learn a simple kata. It might include a punch, a kick, and a block, done to the left and then to the right.

Left: A Japanese martial artist performs a kata at the 2006 Asian Games karate tournament in Doha, Qatar.

As students move up in rank, they learn more difficult katas. Advanced katas have more moves, more complicated kicks, and more difficult hand movements. Usually, students perform multiple katas at their belt tests.

Most karate tournaments have a kata competition, open to people of all ages and ranks. At tournaments, students perform their kata in front of judges. The judges are black belts who will rate competitors on their crispness, power, balance, and strength.

BOARD BREAKING

How do karate students break boards and cement blocks? Breaking boards or cement is always a crowd pleaser. It shows, without a doubt, how strong and focused the karateka can be.

Legend says that *tameshiwara*, the art of board breaking, started in Okinawa. Unarmed Okinawan peasants had to defend themselves against sword-wielding Japanese samurai. According to the legend, the Okinawans learned how to approach a samurai and, with a single punch, break his wooden shield. This legend is a fun idea, but it is almost certainly not true (for one thing, samurai didn't carry shields).

There are two important things a karate student must have to break a board. The first is concentration. Karatekas must believe they can do it. If they doubt their ability to break the board, they will usually pull back at the last moment. When they pull back, they don't punch with all their ability. When a puncher pulls back, the board stays firm, and the fist hits the wood without breaking it. This hurts, and in some cases, can harm the student. It is important that karatekas believe that they can do it. When students are mentally focused and prepared, they will be able to punch with all their might.

The second important thing needed for a successful board break is good punching technique. Instructors start teaching students good technique from their first day of training. The puncher must throw the punch so that maximum force hits the board at just the right time. When the punch is fully extended, the hand should move just past the board. The fist must be tight, with the thumb supporting the first two fingers. When the punching technique is good, the board will likely break. If the thumb or fingers are not in proper position, it is likely that the board will be fine, but the student's hand will be hurt.

Breaking a cement block is much more difficult than breaking a board. It takes more training and more precise technique. People who have not been trained should never attempt to break a board or a cement block. An untrained person who attempts this risks a hand or arm injury.

BASIC PUNCHES, BLOCKS, AND KICKS

Punches start from the hip or the bottom of the rib cage, shooting out straight toward the target. When a punch begins, the palm is up. When the punch finishes, the palm is down. The fist turns over in mid-punch, which provides extra power.

The fist must be tight, with fingers tucked into the palm of the hand. Punching with a loose fist can break a person's fingers. The thumb must be positioned over the first two fingers for support.

Right: The points of impact on a properly thrown punch are the first two knuckles of the fist. The thumb is tucked firmly underneath to protect it and to form a more solid fist.

Left: A reverse knife hand is a good technique for striking soft targets, like the neck, from the side.

Another karate strike is called the knife hand. While the punch comes from the front, the knife hand attacks from the side. The hand is flat, with the fingers slightly turned up. The thumb is tight against the hand. As with the punch, failure to keep a tight hand will run the risk of broken fingers. The knife-hand technique begins near the opposite ear. The palm is facing the ear. Then the arm swings out, and the palm moves to face down as the arm moves.

Right: A martial artist uses an upblock to deflect his opponent's high kick.

An upblock is a defense against a punch or a high kick. The forearm comes across the face, and the karateka's forearm catches the opponent's wrist or leg. The karateka's forearm pushes the opponent's hand or foot up and out of the way. This also exposes the opponent's body. Now, the karateka may counterpunch to the exposed rib cage.

A downblock can be effective against a kick. It pushes the opponent's kick out of the way and usually causes the opponent to be off balance. When the opponent is off balance, it is a good time for the karateka to strike.

Left: A downblock is an effective karate technique against a low kick.

A front kick is the simplest and most basic kick in karate. Facing forward, the student lifts the leg high. The bottom half of the leg swings out sharply. The kick makes impact with the ball of the foot or the heel.

Left: A martial artist executes a high front kick.

Another kick used in karate is the round, or roundhouse, kick. It is much more difficult than the front kick, but greatly adds to the karateka's weapons. In a round kick, the karateka turns to the side, and then points his or her knee at the opponent. The bottom half of the leg swings around, making impact with the top of the instep or the ball of the foot. It is a very fast kick, and an advanced student can direct it with great accuracy.

Right: A black belt karate student executes a roundhouse kick to her opponent's midsection.

Another basic kick is the side kick. In this kick, the karateka turns further around so his or her back faces the opponent's front. Then, the karateka raises the leg, tucking in the knee. The leg shoots out, making impact with the bottom of the heel. While this is a difficult kick to master, it is very powerful and effective.

Karate students learn many ways to strike. The knees, elbows, and even the head can be used as a weapon. Students learn which strikes are most effective, and when best to use them. The strategy is different depending on whether the opponent is large or small, tall or short, or whether there are multiple attackers.

Much of karate training is spent practicing these basic techniques, so that if the student ever needs to use them, they will come naturally, and the student can perform them quickly and effectively.

Right: A well-executed side kick is a powerful and effective strike.

TAE KWON DO

One of the most popular martial arts is a style from Korea called *tae kwon do*. It is not karate, but it shares many of the same ideas, such as a preference for hard, powerful attacks.

Tae kwon do is known for its kicks. Normally, a karate stylist will kick about half the time and punch about half the time. Tae kwon do stylists will kick about three-fourths of the time. Tae kwon do stylists love high kicks, spinning kicks, and leaping kicks.

Tae kwon do officially began after the end of the Korean War in the early 1950s. There were at least nine different martial arts in Korea at that time. Korean martial arts leaders wanted to unify them all under one name and style. They selected the name tae kwon do, which means "the way of kicking and punching," in 1955.

The term tae kwon do has been applied to Korean martial arts for only a few decades. However, Korean martial artists have practiced for perhaps 2,000 years. In early Korean history, the land was split into three kingdoms: Silla, Goguryea, and Baekje. In the kingdom of Silla, a Buddhist monk named Won Kwang Bopsa taught warriors a philosophical and moral code. This code emphasized proper ways of behaving, including loyalty to friends and family. Soon, this combination of academic learning and physical practice became known as hwarang-do.

Above: A pair of tae kwon do stylists spar. Heavy chest shields are needed to protect the fighters from injury when using powerful tae kwon do kicks.

Right: A flying side kick, one of many jumping and spinning techniques used by tae kwon do stylists.

Legend says that the warriors of Silla used hwarang-do to unify the three kingdoms into one country. Some historians say that today's tae kwon do style is an outgrowth of ancient hwarang-do. However, other historians point to the Japanese occupation of Korea before World War II. They suggest that tae kwon do has Japanese and Okinawan origins.

Tae kwon do and karate share wide stances, hard punches, and kicks. However, there are some differences as well. Tae kwon do emphasizes high kicks, jumping kicks, and spinning kicks. Tae kwon do stylists often use the attacker's head for a target, which is uncommon in other styles.

Spinning and jumping kicks are typically not very useful in an actual fight, but they are fun to watch and can have devastating power when executed by a master.

Above: Jesper Roesen of Denmark (left) fights against Myeong Seob Song of South Korea (right) at a tae kwon do quarterfinals match at the 2004 Summer Olympic Games in Athens, Greece. Song eventually won the match. Tae kwon do became an Olympic demonstration sport in 1988 and 1992, and has been an official Olympic sport since 2000.

No First Attack

Below: Two karate students practice on a beach at sunset.

Early in the 20th century, a man named Gichin Funakoshi introduced Okinawan karate to Japan. This popularized the martial art, making it accessible to many people. He wrote a number of books about karate, often from a spiritual or ethical point of view. One of his most famous sayings is, "There is no first attack in karate." This means that karate should be used only for self-defense. No student of karate should ever attack first. This dangerous martial art form is only for defense.

Gichin Funakoshi believed that people who study karate must be very serious. When karatekas study hard, their understanding of karate will flow into all areas of their lives. They will approach everything in life with the same dedication. Most importantly, they will treat everyone with the same respect they have learned in karate.

Above: Serious students of karate make martial arts a part of their lives.

GLOSSARY

Black Belt

The highest colored belt in the ranking system of modern karate. People who earn black belts continue to learn and earn higher ranks, which are called degrees, or dans. A 2nd dan black belt is higher in rank than a 1st dan, and so on.

Empty Hands

The English meaning of the word kara-te, or karate.

Gi

The loose-fitting uniform worn by karate students.

Hwarang-do

In ancient Korean history, a combination of academic learning and physical practice. A possible ancestor of today's tae kwon do.

Karateka

A person who practices and performs karate.

Kata

Also called a form, a kata is a set of prearranged movements, like a dance, that demonstrates a karate student's mastery of the martial arts.

Korean War

A civil war between North and South Korea that was fought from 1950 to 1953. The United States was one of many countries that supported South Korea.

Kung Fu

A Chinese martial art that had an early influence on the development of other martial arts worldwide, such as karate and tae kwon do.

Okinawa

The birthplace of modern karate. The main island of Okinawa is part of the Ryukyu chain of islands, which are situated in the Pacific Ocean south of Japan. Although it was once an independent nation, Okinawa today is a prefecture, or state, of Japan.

Samurai

The trained warrior class of medieval Japan.

Tameshiwara

The art and skill of breaking boards and cement blocks.

World War II

A war that was fought from 1939 to 1945, involving countries around the world. The United States entered the war after Japan's bombing of the American naval base at Pearl Harbor, in Oahu, Hawaii, on December 7, 1941.

Left: A karate student performs a side kick.

INDEX